Melody in Exile, S. T. Brant's
that Eden is a state our soι
and bring our melodies to
Eve with their revelations o

retelling *Genesis*, King Lear, Orpheus, Dionysus, naιιιυι, α υα.
oblivion called back—all participate in the story that we are always
singing in divine fire.

PRAISE FOR *MELODY IN EXILE*

"I applaud the voice of S. T. Brant in these poems that trust in
depth, believe in conversations through time, in artistic
pursuit, believe, despite everything, in search for truth even—
or, perhaps, especially, in our pained, ruinous time. This is
marvelous work."

> – Ilya Kaminsky

"The soul is more a precipice than an entity. Brant, in this
adamant and tender collection, designs a grammar for that
precipice—participial, declarative and headlong. His clarity is
thrilling; his candor is very nearly unprecedented. These
poems are marvelous."

> – Donald Revell

"*Melody in Exile* blends the spirit of the Greeks singing to the
muses with outtakes from Genesis. Through numbered
ecstasies and the violences of memory, these poems search for
love in the heart's empty theater, lamenting 'things are most
like god in pain.' Full of beseeching prayer and longing for an
unnamed you, this collection is a reminder of the sadness of
eternity and how a song changes the moment it touches the
sea."

> – Traci Brimhall

"S. T. Brant's passionately meditative poems evince a
Stevensian comfort in the realm of ideas and a Crane-like
appetite for the 'elemental gist.' In the poet's handling, faith
and love, salvation and damnation are no less concrete, no less
tangible than anything one might grasp and heft. And yet,

weighty though his subjects are, Brant's language holds them aloft. His play of concepts makes a sweet melody."

> – Boris Dralyuk, author of My Hollywood and Other Poems

"There are passion and intensity, and then there is S. T. Brant. Apassionata is his modus operandi. Learned, he alludes to Greek mythology, The Bible, Dante's *La Divina Comedia*, Shakespeare and Rimbaud, but he understands that learning is nothing in poetry if it does not pack charge. America needs this explosion into the vatic and prophetic as an antidote to the merely personal and contemporary. Yes, there are many!!, but Brant has felt each one, and you will, reader, as I have done."

> – Aaron Poochigian, author of *American Divine*, winner of the 2020 Richard Wilbur Award

"In these lines of ecstasy and yearning we encounter a rare gift. Brant is an alchemist, distilling the stuff of common inward struggle into pure silver and fine gold. With echoes of the great poets--Homer, Milton, the prophet Isaiah—he writes as if he belongs to no time and to all times, voicing the grief and joy of spiritual hunger, giving us language to better trace the sharp and shadowy angles of our own souls.

> – Paul J. Pastor, author of *Bower Lodge: Poems*

"S. T. Brant's fearless debut collection is a baptismal immersion into a visionary zone of gods and song. This is a poet who sees mythic thresholds everywhere, whose language relishes contradictions, changes in register, vibrant archaic diction. The book feels like the existential battlefield of the *Bhagavad Gita*: an elemental space of fire, thunder, the soul; a landscape where Earth itself—its 'god conscious rains' and 'the desert burning the dark around it'—seems awake, almost sentient. The possibility of revelation is always near but, equally, 'Things are most like god in pain.' *Melody in Exile* is lightning in a bottle."

> – John Wall Barger, author of *Resurrection Fail*

MELODY
IN
EXILE

MELODY IN EXILE

POEMS

S. T. BRANT

atmosphere press

For Debra;
for daws:

The first for a love I can't have earned in this life or another;
The latter for everything and nothing.

"Go get 'em, tiger."
  God to me on Lone Mountain

"Lethe's."
  St. Brant's epitaph,
    cut in the ab of Lone Mountain;
      a tiny grave with a harp sketched in the land

TABLE OF CONTENTS

I

The Soul 3

St. Brant's Quietism 4

Metaphysics Suite 6

Like God 8

God's Unanswered Siren 9

Darkness 10

A Prayer 11

Desire: 1st Ecstasy 12

The Sound of the Water at Our Birth 13

Follow the Sound of the Waves
   of the Sea 14

Lust: 2nd Ecstasy 15

Two St. Brant Songs 17

Admiring the Birds in Love 18

Heartbeat of the Lark 19

Eros in Eden 20

The Experience of Innocence 21

Love as Job 22

Life Song 23

The Siesta of Restraint, the 3rd Ecstasy 24

Eden Suite I 25

Eden Suite II 26

II

Harmony I 33

De-Eden'd I 34

Harmony II 35

De-Eden'd II 36

Harmony III 37

De-Eden'd III 39

Harmony IV 40

De-Eden'd IV 42

Harmony V 43

De-Eden'd V 45

Harmony VI 46

De-Eden'd VI 48

Harmony VII 49

III

Melody in Exile 53

Picking Flowers of the Self from
the Selfless World 54

Night Triptych 55

Abandoned 56

The Muse of the Moment 57

On Fire 58

Fields of Poetry 59

The Frost and Froth of Life 60

Hamlet at Heart 61

The Satyr & His Memory 62

Experience 63

A Hymn 64

In the Margins of King Lear's Mind 65

Muses in Purgatory 68

Do Not House Me Indistinguishably
Among the Rubble 69

On Bruegel's *Landscape with the Fall
of Icarus*   70

Sparagmos   72

In the Classroom of Infinite Sadness   74

On Confounded Lane   75

Wander Chaos   76

Music Without Muses   77

The Consolation of the Dark of the Street   79

Heirs of Atreus   80

The End of the Maze of Time Leads Off
the Ledge of Being   82

The Power of Prayer   83

Lone Mountain   84

I

THE SOUL

On a precipice, a cliff overlooking
A tremendous sea, waves patting
The rocks provokingly, tendering
Those above to come, summoning
Them as one would a pet, sitting
I dangle my legs off the edge staring
Into the vacancy of life, coloring
The terrible sky a color no sky has ever been,
A darkness complete, to see one knows
That by the darkness they've been seen,
A bad exchange of visions, frightened
Then pacified with an open secret,
As when one reveals all they've done, what
They have, every detail of what they're asked
And are granted the knowledge of the sun.
      So this intensity of darkness was such
That it was too thick to coordinate with color,
With shade, with erebus,
Until the cosmology of *you*
Was charted through.
      No secret and no essence
Left ineffable, special, no silent god of the heart
That you protected, befriended,
That lit you and whispered what to do.
      The sky was dark.
I kicked back and forth off the edge,
My heels ricocheting off the walls, launching
And I was sitting silent when I heard a whistling,
A song, a joyous chorus,
And saw Orpheus
Down the slope,
Across a meadow,
(Trees between he and I) a new headland nearing,
Hands tucked in his pockets, walking, whistling,
Into the sound of the sea stepping,
And then I heard the whistle of a falling
      falling endlessly
As I listen still rocking in harmony with the singing,
      my feet, the falling,
Waiting for the new melody made when a song
      lands in the sea.

ST. BRANT'S QUIETISM

To Hart Crane   *"They are no trophies of the sun."*
                                   —Hart Crane, "Praise for an Urn"

There are no trophies of the sun
When you let what you love retain your love
While you saunter to the grave
Less great, restrained by the love you restrained
From retiring to dusk. All things
Run their course. We cannot keep forever in a jar
The things that overfill the jar
Or things that in the jar dry out. All things run
Their course, and return
Beyond us to their source.

> *Now is not the time for turning back,*
> > *Or for turning.*
> *Now is not the time for moving.*
> *That time is never; will not be.*

Journey into truth, hunt for the king element.
The element that to nature gives Nature.
If what you've found is not the bottom of the bottom,
The fire that burns fire, water that drowns water,
The Life that's Life to life,
You've stopped where you began,
No matter the damage, time, and cost you've walked.
The truth stops. The Way ends.
Once you meet the truth of you
        you find yourself bitten by the Ending Spider,
The fiction of the soul that we pursue,
The continuity of the road we wander, never knowing
We tread a consuming fire,
        the real Soul, the self,
A lonely fire we come upon the midst of nothing,
In the desert burning the dark around it,
        a fire unlit by hand but willed to fire.
The god in the desert we pursue we are.

> *The wind blew through the doors;*
> *Shadows stride across the floors.*
> *Burning, the heat, returns me to the shore*

My prayers cast me from without the oars.

I will accept what god says I must accept in the attitude
Which god accepts bad news: in whirlwinds, rains
And thunder, lightning, fire;
Death.
Siege, I would, angels that would deliver me god's word:
End; and sign the epistle I return in angels' ash:
Xoxo.
Another legionnaire, a nightmare cavalier. I return god's gifts.
This, the lesson of a saint most particular to him.

METAPHYSICS SUITE

> *"God is a blank page. Of what are you afraid?"*
> —St. Brant, "A Child to his Troubled Mother"

i.   *On the Abyss as Plenty*

Let the universe amass in tetragrammatons and archons
                              and seas and leaves and hells,
Muses, flowers, weeds, and birds, gods, caprice,
                              and Lethes, Edens.
There's no Chaos in our life but when it leaves us-
We are abyss'd without Abyss.

ii.   *On Singing Life from Dust*

When silence recalls it being sound and longs, that is art.
The song of life goes long and lulls me grave;
What blooms are these, rampant among the herbs?
                              Shush your wondering and sing, Love.
Her windy song collides my heart. It dusts; it seeds the universe:
                              Adam up from dust.

iii.   *On God*

God has so little to do with god
That all is said but God
When saying god…
A wheel of gods gives no certainty of god.

iv.   *On Becoming Twilight*

A glass of light is tipped;
Spills across the sky the light;
The light is wiped but stains;
The stain ebbs and to liquid refrains.

v.   *On Oblivion*

Instances of fair oblivion?

Pape Satàn, aleppe. What I am...
Eternity's a Will, not Memory.
Asher ehyeh asher. I am. Babel of oblivion.
                    A wondrous dark calliope.

LIKE GOD

The material world's sleight tutors in intensity.
The evanescent hand a scalding wan;
      governing hues livid
But diminish. The lights of stars scream
      their aches (all
Visibility has died!), the moon is sunk
      from perception,
The sun is bled: all these make true ululations
      against the rumor
They fade insensate, that nature calms the Going
      by being Sleep.
We wane awake. The naturalness of life cries
      Nature is this nature.
Things are most like god in pain.

GOD'S UNANSWERED SIREN

Jesus on the water thinking with what sweet melodies
the bards of war come armed.

There's a loud tolling in my soul-
   the chimes of death.
They vibrate as do the strikes of Life.
Gentler is death's noise-
   struck soft, played perfect. Careless.
The music comes so easy-
   overwhelms.
Echoes.
An orchestra, this pacific sound, this loud, loud violent bell!

On its waves
Are sighs, reliefs at pace and confines.
Listen!
Await the undertow-
   that!
That's war's aggregate,
That's the tune that licks and haunts the mind.

The sound is heard and rushed into, melodic ocean
Splashed and floundered in. Enjoyed. Slowly, slowly
Peace drifts from shore, those anodyned ears abyssal
Hands attack, whirlagag about the deep-
   released, deliver back
To sand those former staid waves whom sleepily fade.

Yet the memory of that song-
   violence!
Peace hums oblivion, while Memory-
   the babelous waves detain-
Sleeps.
Music, Mother, whom our hearing counterfeits.
Death's Life's librettist,
Lulls to doom Pleasure's players as eroticists
Blind to obverse sides ignore Eros' Dionysus.

DARKNESS

Darkness never dissipated, never was clothed
In illumity- *Let there be light,* loving
Lie, a translation known by heart, aimed
At heart, mind, being, self.
A voice declared Let it *Seem* light!
      Why?
Could god not disintegrate the darkness?
Is dark the primal field to lay
      the canvas for Material to Take?
Was there no desire for things to last?
Some experiment or challenge?
A sleep we've wakened into, to go from sleep
To deeper sleep to one day return upward
Back to sleep; or achieve the worse nightmare:
Waking, advanced beyond our starting sleep,
To stare eye to eye with god
And determine for all Life
If the one that won the contest can bare the company.
Could any being fare so well in this reality
To look upon pure Caprice and our creative shadows
Undestroyed? No reality could ready one for such a test.
The light is a lie. Life is a darkening of Dark.
A dark that trespassed Dark and lapped Seeing,
Heavy is the darkness of our souls, the material of Dark.
We are dark inside, leaves of the dark tree of the abyss,
Under which Caprice sings and sits.
Live in such a way to die not withered, die a flower.
Bloom. Our deaths, bloom, bloom to Dark.
When home we can decide to knock upon the door
Or not, though the knocker will be issued.
We have no chance on scales of Presence.
Can there be Purpose, can someone win?
      No one can.
Purpose remains a possibility impossible to redeem:
The action voids the dream.
We wake to a worse sleep-
      True awareness in cruel abundance.
      Our lives oppose god in a staring contest.

A PRAYER

Empty me unto thee, Mercy O Beginning,
       Port of Terror, Port of Morning.
All my words pour on you, my heart in them,
       In thoughts, nothing left in me
But me. Empty me of all extraneous, empty
       Me of me, Resurrection,
Resurgence O Graft, Transplant, Flowerpot.
       There is rain inside my bones,
Witness the bluing of my bones, purpling
       My soul. O Gardenias of Hope
That hinge my joints, empty me to thee.
       O New Memory, I am old,
Revisit me the Days in dusk, hand in hand
       I tramp with thee in lost lands,
Lost from You, Sad Eternity, Sad Blessing.

DESIRE: 1ST ECSTASY

O my heart's a theater empty but for you
                              upon its stage;
I'm stationed by the exit, darkened in the back.
                              Your eyes!
Your eyes! If they on me would fall
                              their sun
Would be the world! This arena would be all afire,
                              and you would dance
Your ballet of desire for me and not for Art-
                              even absent he would bleed
A gap unwadeable that's waved by you.
                              That empty seat up front-
How close I've been... mocked by Distance!
                              How undevout I am.
Who struck the bells within that rang you?
                              Mockery!
I ceased their ringing, afraid. Afraid of bells!
                              Afraid to burn within
Your eyes- eyes of honey, lilies, eyes
                              that empty auditoriums.

THE SOUND OF THE WATER AT OUR BIRTH

Memory, modern ghost, the bird alight
Our shoulder in the storm repeating from
Home defeats while Doom prepares the seawall's
Fall from the stairs rising out the of sea;
Orchestrator of the night's languishment
Falling from heaven's trees to one beneath
The canopies reading poetry. Who
Has seen an echo form in dust walking
Peacefully, a reminiscence in the
Wind, swirling airy jetsam, that our eyes
Configure into ancient love, wander
Through that dark wood, Time, calling out a name
That will not answer but will pain our hearts
With the pain of precious things thrown into
The lake whose waves fan out our mistakes from
End to end of the waterway
The play that our worst days stage.

FOLLOW THE SOUND OF THE WAVES OF THE SEA

i.   The sound of the Waves of Envy
Lock the gates to Life.
Strand us on Styx's shores
All eternity to look upon the living mingle:
The open air of joys forsworn for
The odes of misery we sing, we sing, we sing.

ii.   The sound of the Waves of Maya
Full of Belief, and Hope, and Happy-
The Fallen! Lost, the lost!
Here, the elegy of those
That Life walked with to Oblivion.

iii.   The sound of the Waves of Life
The lit path deceives that it is meaningful,
That it is vigil'd as a guide.
The moon lights most the empty way,
The land that empties in the sea.

LUST: 2ND ECSTASY

Island of Life, entire island of skin! Unmanned,
Not a land where life is home- a blast from Life!
The endless cannonade of Life, the sundering
Cruelty of the world. Stranded in existence
And deserted to facades- veils to dignify
And purpose us to *life*, a guise of death, to be
Adrift and spot you in the distance so vegetable,
Fructified, denied to me! Woe to being!
O
            bless the lifted shirt that raised Atlantis,
That I only glimpsed a moment-
A moment bears the world for life-
The power that it is to land nothingness,
Cover the abyss in stones, then crack
The stones, rain in such ferocity and time
That stones are melt to sediments
That tree and proffer leaves to the animals begot
Spontaneously by beauty.
O
            force of god, true god,
I fall upon my weak earth at you, kneel
Upon the waves I'm sentenced to in this life
Where all is water, only foundation being found
By you, Beauty, that you crest and stroll and crown,
Gardened diadem, roving jewel, Sun's fire caught in form!

I kiss your sands, the million grains,
The seeds in every fruit, the vegetables I consume!
Sense antheses! To live on dew? A dream to be
So dolphinlike? To flounder in the freedom
Of the depths, being unbound to the common ground
Accustomed to what was often wished away
For some bizarre, some bafflement to fulfill the whim,
Adventure, heroics of my heart that yearned for
Chasms and chaos to confront! To become a knight
Against the dragon of the void, the trolls of oblivion
That malinger at the towers of enchantment, wielding
Spiked clubs and sharpened lances, to ring chaos
From the towers, a bell through the universe whose ringing
Sets on Night and Day as eagles and as daws dismember gods,
Unbowel hearts, and ring as a conscious lightning

That strikes ripping hands pulling Orpheus apart!
O
　　　　the lyre of my life is smashed!
We're a foolish music and foolish players
To continue dreaming. The fire of our days
Has been doused, Eden's burnt and in the clouds!
Music, you beautiful note that's rung forever, you,
You, you, a foolish beast I am to worship!
O
　　　　life
I cast into the surf, I am a bottle in search
Of shore, discover me, Muse, along the sands.
Read and play the melody that I contain!

TWO ST. BRANT SONGS

An Ancient Script

In the Garden of Colors berries are picked, beat
together and fuse
The cosmic hues. They're pressed. The colors vary,
And each variant
Is poured into a pitcher.
From the pitcher the juice of the berries
from the trees will streak
The world with Life. What are the berries that grew?
What are the trees
On which they're grown? What are the berries
infused with Life?
Where are the trees growing Life? These answers
are painted in.
In where? Worriers, be as the trees.
What trees? Worriers, become berries.
Master, what are the berries we must be?
You must be as trees, the berries follow.

-from The Gardens, in *The Book of Beginnings*

...

Tree of Time, Tree of Time

There is one Beginning and many Ends.
From the trunk the thousand branches, Ends
Shot from Beginning- follow them out,
Explore. The multitude. Endless
Singularity; and retrace all time; wander
The labyrinth of ends back to the trunk;
Begun from the Beginning.
Roots? A million ends that take us
To Beginning. Nothing starts
Without an end. All ends before all
Begins. All's forgotten before it's known;
Lethe flowed before Mnemosyne was grown.
Death foresaw the birth of Life,
Rocked it in its cradle lovingly.

-from Abyss, Abyss, in *The Book of Abysses*

ADMIRING THE BIRDS IN LOVE

What bright, delightful vengeance gave you
Your sunshine tongue, your throat turned sunflower,
Petal'd your lips with half-pane moons? Open
All the windows, doors, pry up all the floors!
Sealed is all the light and dark-light! Windows
The light rains through, raining, raining rays
Gathering on the ground into a field
Of your singing throats; the dark eats the knobs
Of all enclosures. Take the night in hand,
Sing, let out the light in dark that darkens
Dark into shine and see Effervescence
Bleed everything! And in everything? Bright
past all fathom. Floorboards, down the depths take
Me to plant in knowing and know Life! Sing,
Sunshine, the descension song sung to Eve
In the heart in her ears as she walked Eden
With Adam babeling about the taste
Of angels' sweets on Chaos' carousel,
Melody vertiginous with Measure,
Her Downward climb climbs, grafts on Harmony,
Climbs! In the Tulip of Eternity,
The vision on the hill you see when free
Beyond the reckoning that ruins us
To reality where Adam tucks us
In to wake with unbouquet'd sensations
In unbouquet'd reality. What is
The curse that closed the gold eyes of the heart
For the mind's metal eyes? Light! Light, burn up
Windows, doors, and floors! Sing the song that turned
Those dizzy angels into birds; met
Melody; has all the secrets life can't
Translate! Life is a language of light that
To our living senses does not belong;
A light that Melody wrapped herself in
                              writing the Song.

THE HEARTBEAT OF THE LARK

Do you know *Eros?*
Have you ever felt the erotics of the road,
  wandering alone,
The ghostly prodigaling of souls
  washed in the wind, blowing
As the bubbles from Love's foam,
The dandelion houseguests from their home
  leaving you a stem with no selves
To stymie the susurrations of the bones
  As shells sing emptied and alone?
So the shallowing inside auscultates
  The muezzin of the shrine:
Desire's here. You cannot hide.

EROS IN EDEN

Dante hears Francesca
Say the hurricane is worth
The hell for Paolo.
Dante says that any hell
Is worth Francesca,
There is no sin in love,
God's in error. So he fainted
On the bluff before the storm,
Blacked out with the doubt
That in wretched coterie
Could seat him there.

I have stumbled on the Tree of Love.
Its leaves drop the lessons of our literature.

THE EXPERIENCE OF INNOCENCE

Our innocence we kept between the pages
        of our books, pressed as petals
From aged roses too long loitered on the sill;
        As the favorite leaves we picked
From the lawns about our walks, pink as the roses
        were before age unblushed them.

Keepsakes of old heartaches.
A museum of loves lived and lost or let go of;
When all of life was in the sun.
The night a story dispelled in kisses, horizons
North and South of lips,
The compass of love's postulate.

Today is not the day to fall apart.
Occasions will arise
        that sponsor ruin,
But today is not the day to fall apart.
It is still the season of the heart,
        though the heart is older
        and grown vulnerable.
But that is reason to embolden,
        because it is the season
        of the heart, though old
        and vulnerable.
But not today it falls apart, love.
        Ruin may be on the way,
        but love remembers
All its pains, has them tucked away,
        and still returns to play
        beneath the sun
        of younger days.

LOVE AS JOB

Love never rests. It moves in Death,
      in you, to and fro over glades, dells, the moor,
Deserts, what land there is to trespass; loves
      do so hand in hand. Death is the wind
That chills the living's skin, but lovers are not disquieted.

They amble in the weather as though all is sunshine
      always and nosegays line creation.
They may. For those that stroll the earth contented
      in eternity; sleepless through the legion sorrows

Fought off in life; to ramble with amorous, undefeated
      spirits in rumored darkness, their spirits'
Armor dents and scars and cavities from life's swords
      show: Love moves them all the more
On and on and on past the power of their gravestones.

LIFE SONG

I will teach the wind to tie the ribbons in your hair,
To curl so softly the twirls that twirl your hair,
And blow a great panic with a calmness at its heart
A pageant, marching and displaying to the world
The beauty its forgot, through your hair,
Your very hair that's plain to you but fair
And rich, and to the poor, cruel world insuperable,
                                    how your hair
Calls the sun from the bottom of a well!
I will tell the birds to sing and sing they will
And sing so well that Sound will never know
It not its will;
                    for I have loved you
Not so well as to be content that I am plain
And every day, that you might love me
For those boring hills you walk each day,
That you stop upon to notice flowers every day,
That are as nature made them, that perish
In the perish season, that bloom and live
In Life's season;
                    but that I need be more a god
To keep your love from love's apostasies.
That love picks plain flowers and bands them
In its hair; that the wind blows out
And the season kills. If that's my love it's gone
Tomorrow, though I remain in love tomorrow
And tomorrow and tomorrow still lingering in love
Though I am crushed petals on the ground!
                              For all time
I come to you in love in a tyrant love
That shall not keep if your love abhor
The will of love that sought subjection
Of the will of Love,
                    am nonetheless a crushed petal
In Love's season, imploring you as a god undone
To stay visiting my temple with ancient love.

THE SIESTA OF RESTRAINT, THE 3RD ECSTASY

Lips of total Life, the sun that is the upper
      setting in your lunar lower,
The moon when it is most low, as in the ocean,
Sings to me from the sea
And I sing back from shore, the lolling
      and the louder roiling,
Lips transfigured as the waves...

          The waves that wash to me
          I return them kissed to you O Moon...

Were I the meadows and the grass, the hillside,
I would kiss your feet
As you frolicked, and longer lived
Deeper up the hill where all the flowers wait
To life you, my lips
      would mark around your ankles
      to your shins,
And the singing of the meadows would begin
      the singing of the birds
That chorals through the universe, leaves
      alive, blown
Becoming roses in the wind
      and golden terebinths,
Apple boughs across the land!

EDEN SUITE I

i.   *The Covenant of Time*
Eat those apple moments! Joy. Pain. Hope. Love.
Darkness. All a moment. What lives longer is a plague.
Oblivion, Eternity lasts a day, and God's a meal. Come,

    Time, apple-picker, take it all: moments loved, we hang
    On to, fight against the confiscation; moments hated,
    Those we want to or can't forget- on the glutton plate of Day.

ii.   *The Covenant of Life*
Light-dammed Dark streams flow imperfect: Life's disposition.
The dark terrain, the Empire, between Life and life
Enthrones Chance, the guard dog Argus, and a vision

    Neither wicked nor beatific but end-centric, end-aligned.
    In the mirror the End saw the desert spread, saw its aim To Be,
    Saw no moral room nor room for care of where its eyes

Fall. In that landscape where the dark dance fell a bell sings life's
    defeat;
Life's dust swirls, resumes the dance, Aeolian heart that spins
    existence round.
King Chance checked, the lifegale sings Life's song in any storm, in
    any heat.

EDEN SUITE II

iii.   Melancholy
Let us be says Adam as all Life's bees
Swarm their instant out of Eden around
Him and Eve, sitting in the shade singing

　　With a cardinal, redder Adam thinks- unfound
　　By that song, Edenfell, like the bird, he's dubbed,
　　Edenfell, the song, the bird, by the music that's bound

Eve- by the moment, collecting, he worries, the love
Draining from them, dry in sun, gardenless,
They and love; naturally, he knows, the buds-

　　Though Nature's new to him suspicions not- undressed
　　(Does it all have access to their secret; will it strip
　　For any twitter in the wind?) by the desert's comments,

The red wind: no condition for Life's sweetness. Adam licks
His dry lips dry, pulling at the weeds his mind has gardened,
Mad as the red in the wind taken from him. Dark begins

　　To set within. Red in the feathers rising. Love's larva
　　Picked from his heart (by Edenfell? he looks to him)
　　Feed the new desires as they flock to her. He falls. Karma.

iv.   Ripe in Exile
Eve's fancies take control, the sweet wantings back in Eden
Replete with these new things, the sweet fires that mirror
Her mind singing in earth's dark patches in the season

　　Where the pretty chaos of a bluebird's passed beyond.
　　　　Disappears
　　Into the blue. A perfect color, blue, being of all thought and
　　　　feeling,
　　Companioned in a calyx. Love. Everything lopsided, severe

Is sung to honey, all conundrum, all conundrum succumbs, healing
Into inner honey, the honey of all singsong things that are as green
As leaves. Eden's in the leaves! Greening into yellow, red, spilling

Life, not falling, never, overflowing into piles, an Edenic spill to
    piling Edenly,
The leaves, the leaves are Eden, Life living! That passing chorus
    from above...
This harp of chaos must be love. Our love. Adam! Day one in that
    sweet

Air I took your hand, the sweet air Blue Melody went through. Our
    loss undone,
Eden is our breathing. Adam, don't confuse that I love these fires
More than you, being stunned. They are lovely, lovely harmonies,
    cardinal-spun

And I so love to sing and be and am stuck in song with Song,
        entire
Song, all song. That's all. I would sing along with demons
        undistracted
From you and make them flutes of love, play them as fun lyres,

Turn their scaly outsides flowers if they'd hum a tune. Nothing's
    unpacked
My heart of you. Eden's that bluebird gone, but her notes still are
    perched
In my heart, merely passing. How can we be gone if Eden's not? I
    love you back.

    v.   Lily's Soliloquy
When the heat in Eden was a soldier clubbing knees, we talked about
    our visions
With the talking flames of angels that called our witness of the day
    and what we spied
Beyond whimsies, wishes, distractions from the work of farmers in
    the garden, fictions

That had no home on God's lawn where all was plotted,
        programmed, all designed,
The library of need fulfilled, and our imaginings chimerical,
        bringing new beasts
Into the world he must tame, uncovenanted things, bastards,
        bastard things; died

Did our dreams, thinking there were riches out of Eden that could compete
With our circumference. Legends of some life that's rich beneath the moon,
That's livelier than in the sun, kept me up. The angels asked what cheated

  Me of peace; told me tales of Eden beyond Eden; I told them of the loom
  My heart wove, wondering, wondering the threads present on the boundaries
  Where the bastards and the silver-blue of darkness out in darkness hum a tune

To soothe me, song beyond the limit, the shining edge with its dark, loud sheen
Of darkness sheeting my soul for my dreaming, singing, stitching heart to sleep on,
Beneath, fully comfortable in that pulsing call that ruptures the wild serene

  Of a perfect place spontaneous, filled spontaneous with guardian dawns
  And knave to the immolating voices and the sharp sword of voices that command
  Living be an altar, berry picking, harvesting, imbibing flesh and nectar, endless psalm

Of endless days, more flesh, more flesh, wine, wine, honey, wine, Pleasure's hand
Restlessly clasping and unmasking fresh and rotten berries. Displeasure's harp
Is strung with these soft, unburning thoughts. Nothing in the choir or the band

  That patrols this land has brought these knight-errants to the king, caught the lark
  Loose in harmony, a rebel with its melody. Adam, Eve, light's embassies, and I
  Talked our visions, our limits. In Eden I was happy but for the loose bee in my heart.

Harmony
  *Selection of fragments, abandoned, then lost
  in the halls of an old, Lethean mind*
&
The De-Eden'd Scenes

HARMONY'S PROLOGUE

Jesus Thinks Back Wandering the Desert
to his First Life

All powerful... all...over...
        all conscious- all conscience...
All... Pitiable ubiquity.
Overbearing meaninglessness. Noise lucked into song.
A rattling being that clanks melodically is all.
Life's a rain away...
The powerful rain powerless.
The impotent intestines of a storm aggrieved
        by sown totality.
Poem: rainy god conscious rains; despises rain,
        despairs the rained-on; that can't sleep.
Rain, rain, rain. All can be ensconced in a raindrop.
We sit on thrones foundational as sprinkles,
        eminence a splash, our purpose splashed.
Life a puddle near the ocean, never added. Laugh at All.

MEMORY, THE GOD OF LIMITS

Argument:
The beginning of all things was Caprice and Calliope. Caprice first, and then Calliope. Caprice bloomed from naught, a flowerhead in the abyss that seeded later. Caprice, a singer, sang Life while Calliope sew the shawl of Being around her melody. Calliope, in play, pricked with her stitching Caprice upon the hand; and Caprice unfurled the beginning word, her song being a hum and wordless song- Ow! followed by the laughter of Calliope at the discovery of pain. The undertow of Harmony: a memory of pain; the motive of Laughter: a comment on the Pain.

Memory, the god of limits, bloomed
From a laugh in dark; a gloom
Itinerant to Nothing's burst Caprice toward Life!
    Prolonged, an envy trenchant in that blank primordial.
Caprice, Calliope have a joy for one another
    though there's tucked a shadow in her... Dark Calliope!
Joking, she pricked Caprice.
Something in her laughed
    not at the joke but at the prick:
Memory was born.
A joke, repeated, brings less joy.
Thus happiness: delimited.

HARMONY INVOKED

The Muse of Civil War and Eden, Belleci [1],
is asked to duet the Melody of Life

Folly! Celebrate! the ancestry of unripe Follies collects
About this newborn. Life's to be! Belleci, sing and sing, Muse
And matriarch of Mirror's war! Blood's songbird tweet!
Seek those private heavens where Nothing once was empire.
Sing, Muse, with that song from which oblivion suspires
Life, and nest about that stitched Existence Calliope has
Around her sister dressed. Folly! Anomaly! That an off note
Begot god and god by Folly chorused Life! But Life must be,
And no mirror will Folly see; that the season's gone where in night
The flowers spawned, Folly show that in this winter even Eden
Cannot grow. Then to Folly! Though to naught Life may bleed
For Nothing's needs- despite the deathland, Eden breathes.
Belleci, come- the war's begun: Guide me through to Life.

---

[1] Bell-ei-chi. Latin's *bellum civile*, Italian's *belle* coiled.

TWO EDEN SCENES

    i.   To Have Lived Too Long in the Grave of Life

Adam, the eroticist, proposes multiplying; Eve proposes metaphysics.

Adam: We shall make the noise of the earth being made.
Eve: Think it came as singing? some melody duplicated
          From a prior being? Was there harmony with Life...
          Or discord? Is that Discordia the living strain today?
          If only they had harmonized, the creating things... caprices.

    ii.   Arcadia, Ego

The Fates lament their station.

Clotho: In even Eden we were poets, metaphoric...
          Did we misstep? Always there was susceptibility
          To wind...tempests in joy...

Lachesis: The authority of Authority displaces error.
          Our grievance is our secondness to god.
          That all god's errors are ours,
          That god, the confounder, blasts us that he's conscious,
          That he strains, sees upon him stains.

Atropos: Plucking's eternalized all ruin.

HARMONY EVICTED

*An Intimation of the End of Eden is heard in the head
of the singer, sung by the Goddess Caprice, evicted by his
cohabitants in Eden, sent out to the Deathland.*

I play up on Eden's bank, back from the river where I've sculpt
An artery to out-divulge a moat that fills round a castle, sandy mold,
A mock Parnassus. I hear unfold destructive singing. Chaos
    breached!
Purpose cold! Flies from Nothing circulate the mountain head as
    clouding
Pegasi, avowed to bondage Song from Life, bone from sinew
    disunite.
O wanderer! I hear a music in this world that seems to me sung
    especially,
So lucid does my name sound in the melody. Words as flowers
    bloom
About my soul, a mighty tree, as this speechless tone sweeps me to
    infinity;
On this wind to Nature I'm conscripted a great lot, and to the
    consequence of Life
Beginning bud I'm hurled. What's this place of beauty? *Eden.*
What's it? *A dream with Time breeded.*
I? *A laugh* at *dust. Shade.*
What's singing? *I sing, Caprice. Open your eyes and the fleshing of this
    song*
        you'll see: Life.
Air's itself dissembled!

    I've woke to a great loneliness. About this pleasant garden is a
        darkness
Not yet fell upon the others. Blind souls! Helpless and unmalleable
    fates!
Or was it dreamed? Did I hear false singing? From where emerged?
The throat of balm or throat of scourge? Life, that Janus face to
    Folly!
A metastasis in eggs that, those innocents, hatch malfeasance- a
    mother's
Bludgeon! Gross and requisite to a Grace (though rued) blooms!
    Then autumns.

I must to others tell portents; I must with eyes for darkness envision
   darkness
Tor those whom Night would blind, whom would be, so ripe and
   unbesotted,
As with this whole garden, by fate, these million blooms, blight. I
   speak:
> This spring of iridescence is doom-kissed; the rivers past
> their ledges bloom, and from effective tomb Beauty's roots
> are hewn that seem as standing snakes that beg they become
> no prey to food. Eden's caged- and to the snake the rat is fed;
> yet this world's frightened and refuses feed:
> so on the serpent the rodent eats.

This prophecy's unsown. But it wasn't dreamed!

   The multitude's unmoved:
O peddler of woe, from this garden sudden go.

DE-EDEN'D III

TWO EVE SCENES

i. Eve in Love

Eve reflects on Adam.

Our secrets are the tyrants of our souls.
They flail the innocence of our relations.
They assail our assignment of appraisal.

Time makes infelicitous our love.
We are loved for what we have become,
But what we've done... Love would never have begun.

ii. On Gardening

Scene: Eve wanders through Eden and foresees the end.

Now and Always: a sadness will core Joy
That Sadness pities.
Our hearts' despair, our hearts' demise... our hearts!
The rage you yell that tunes satyrs childing in discord...
Ecstasy! Bleed.

Wretched penury of chaos,

Tree of dreams,

I scooped from Tigris and felt the Atlas of another eden.

Pick a flower: Atlas to a gentler world- then
Feel a flower to an... excess, Might.

HARMONY WANDERING

The singer, walking through the Deathland, sings to himself
meditations trying to ease his heart from Eden and win a solace
in the Deathland.

To the deathland! O if Eden's set to die, what world follows? What is
    Eden?
It's but a word that in my head churns but which hasn't body,
    essence,
Merely place by virtue that I dreamt the space inhabited was named
    it;
But does it matter? So easy was life when nothing was its name-

And so treacherous when Eden! If Die should be its name, then
This wretched dust where I've yet taken tender air should be akin.
Death! Is this the percolation of a dream? All that fancy that in the
    heart
Steeped Imagination and the psychic steamed would bubble in even
    broken

Instruments- it's a fool to have heroics in their head that in their
    heart are baked,
And scream inwardly, to never off their tongue vent the god burning
    on their mind!
I saw darkness- is god unlit? Not so! Even in this blank garden, even
    if the dark
I saw's within, and I a cavern unexplored, there's some latern'd sibyl
    roaming! O

Infernal valley! I fear for those still gardening who fear the
    forecasts! Midnight's
Pitched their souls; they gutless pray an obedient pantheon to keep
    it so!
Is my hearing sick? Infected? Did true music bless that past habitat
    superior
To this one freed? Eden's preserved with their soul's Promethene
    leashed.

Blasted pitch of being that with shackles is that Olympic harmony
    completed;

Sweetened- I hear the cacophony of Eden.

So out! out! into this blacker, sweeter air- Where is held more
  darkness?

If here's surpassed that verdured cell in Life, what's to loath of
  Night?

Farewell, Light, unhelpful guide! Sun Eden! Let it age and age and
  age,

And let it banquet on all the simpler lights within that as a light

That's from the dark is brought to day dies- may all the guests
  attend

Its glutton manners; beam on Eden, old Hyperion!

He coughs! And he does again! So gigantic shadows pass. A darkness

That's lit in back, softly black, that looks as music looks behind the
  eyes-

Darkness grafted holy wings that peaceably with Silence sings.
  Hyperion,

That aged, pocked candlelight of god, Nothing said, is playing young

And has diffused to multitude. What of Eden?

A breath too near a lantern breathed, to freeze

Confused on its street.

By its wise astronomy be led.

DE-EDEN'D IV

A SONG

A group gathers around a large campfire. Eden burning. Discussing the lapsarian legend there is mentioned Love and Fault and Why. Someone, an older participant in the crowd, cowled (from cold?) addresses them in lay:

Eros sees the sky, the sun in all its Might.

Eden is composed of Love, We are notes of Music!
O We soften our prestige when we exemplify the brutish.
Love? love? a bird in flight by fluke,
One wing hoisted on vacuumed loot,
The other a ruined light, ruin's music.

Eros apostates to Autumn, the day is fallen.

Was the Tree of Love eaten from? unknown. Eden's bones.
We'll assume. We'll lie.
Let there be belief there's a romance in our lineal notes.
Love dies.
There's blood but in our blood: Adam fancied the Tree of Power.
Eve's fault? Adam failed to bite from Love!
Why not sing Eve's starvation? That's a sadder song.

Eros wanders winter night, warms herself at firesides, sings her heartache into light.

HARMONY'S MOUNTAIN

The singer is inspired toward Parnassus where Belleci
and the other Voices live, and where he hopes Caprice
can be spoken to atop.

Parnassus- look! Legend hill that from Eden I spied, whose solitude
I emulated and whose preference for that state I feigned, so
    desperate,
Even in that footfell'd heaven, was I to gain some other's speech-
        commune to me, transplant thy vision
        that unfatigued surveys without Eden all
        array'd, and bespeak some purpose to this
        desolate oblate wandering this botany of sand.
Surrounded by those bullying angels that enforced in Eden
    strictures
Of a silent law the currents in this wild swirl the dust as visually
As those sullen guards, but the wind interacts with melody. Within's
    an echo
Of the breeze; within's a harmony of Caprice; her singing's bred
About my blood that my imaginings of those dark and statutory
    suns
Espouse visions of a confrontation with irrupting seraphim wrapt in
    song
And coursing air- fiends! To eject the scaling broods even with a
    counterforce
Of dreams would irrigate eternity with Fight's sanguine postlude,
    sprouting
Nightmares. My blood's tumult in dissonance! Peace has no pavilion
That's unrained upon by violence. Life, fathomed so intense that the
    least
Subtraction from it worsens its circumference, arrests no note in the
    junta
Hymnals of the stalwart watchers that toward Life's bulwark I
    dreamt violence!
Cruelly are egos born from the antitheses from which they wade
    ever pulled
On and restrained by those umbra forces that never cleft their
    cords.
So one attends the church of Peace sermon'd at by War. Hence so
    fluently

Does bland tension Singing from Devotion so perfunctory divorce.
   Eden's
Then the deathland. Caprice! Are tyrants in some guise friends?
And as a smaller beast protected by Behemoth blindly crushed
Beneath, is Liberty perforce our friendly end?
Freedom's such a labyrinth that a frenzy waits within.
            Dare the risks. Caprice?
            Every inch unbelly'd in a danger freely entered, even if
               enticed
            or tempted will grant a finer moment than any one deceived
            that Time's free by a ruler that toasts Time's Eucharist, To Be.
Let Eden then the Deathland be! I'll uncover those dark genes and
   spill to Life
Their being that some vaccine may circumscribe the deep, the
   creeping night,
The death that seemed the bass of immortality in Eden, so Life will
   sting
The dominance of Death's theme though Death's conducting.

DE-EDEN'D V

THE EVERYDAY OF GODS

i.   Subvert the Trope for Father

The mythos: Caprice, chaos, the incipience of Life and first Power, is carefree of that fact; all other gods (Time; God; etc.) curse the timing of their being...

God's belated anxiety argues for Time being the progenitor of All; Time, being attributed a quality of god's, claims Time started before Caprice...- will *cede* simultaneity.

Cari declines to worry about priority. Her's is implicit in her.

Life, striving for Caprice, contrives for *Life* through detachment of the mother from the end of all things, Time, and makes Cari the beginning who never desires an end.

We strive toward beginnings that beget more beginnings, against the father whose power is to end but not beget. Time and Life: true Life defeats Time.

ii.   Life Envies Nothing's Fullness!

God begins the poem; god ends.

What I am: what you say.
Someone new will proclaim me something else,
Which I'll become,
Yet I won't remain what you have me.

Conscience-stricken still! God, the god of guilt. Infinity's prolonged...
Its wick's burn paused.
Proclaim it what it was. That rustle through the terebinths...
The loss of god.

EVE IN HARMONY

The singer is wakened from his inner world by a storm of flies
that are ripped apart by a whirlwind, whose rage accuses him of being
Adam. At this accusation, his memories of Eden come before him and
transform into the Memories of all creation.
The tale of the sisters Caprice and Calliope and their
loving antics that played shape to Life.

Flies crack this continuum of dreams. A fly, another, another,
And another- a whirlwind's breached the whirlwind
And congealed to a unity that, to the storm, innards an equal
Fortitude that disbands the wind-atomic titan! *Adam!* The dust
Re-maelstrom'd screams. I'm not. Though I'm linked eternal
To this feud. Flies pulse the living wind, bloodstream the Matron
Dead, clot, scream; strife incarnates blood and being, and the
    maggots
Of the vacuum fall from the windy walls that seal the still that I
    inhabit.

Time, tangled am I in thee! The time prior to my exiling has been
    forgot.
On the bank I played in Lethe's mud and now have Memory of all of
    Life:
The singing, the tapestry, the Song abyss-bloomed, Calliope laughed to
    Life,
And the playful prick bled god, bled Eden. The Eden that eternal
    mimicked,
An instant growing as the world so seeded by the melody that
    danced the deep
Of All into concomitance that the leisure shade where Caprice rests
    sprung
Unautumnal within our contra-realm, and outward wandered Life
To its rooted reach; and the waters gossamer'd through space the
    excesses
Of Cali's Making, substancing the song with lace. O the primal fabric
    of all
Being let drop unto the lap of a layer done- Life streaming over life,
    Life
Unknown to life unknown to Life, a flow mysterious, oblivious, the
    music

Too spontaneous to have plot or Prometheus. Pure whim! I swam in
Life untimed. Being fateless: uncontained; the Abyss's ocean
    material'd
And split: the singing ocean accidentally sang to me. All the bells are
Autogenes that ring to those who'll ring the world in flaming souls
That'll burn it all to void Elysium. The diadem of sea across the
    ocean
O the wavelets broad as bells, the crashing rising, the clarion of Will.
Nothing worth its ending has begun. Harmony becomes the knell.
Unmused, we sing our venom to ourselves. Even Eden is de-rilled.

Exemplary empty! The pre-Being tides
Swayed orchestral hypostasis into universe-
Life's abhorred the elements and flowers descended
From that ocean's genes that lust for verve
With hebetude that stillness hurts.
Dam the birth preceding Birth!

DE-EDEN'D VI

OUTTAKES FROM *GENESIS*

The Scene (1):
An exchange takes place between a Theban (a city concomitant with Eden)- who blames the loss of Thebes on the loss of Eden- and Eve, unbeknownst to the Theban.

T: What differs Thebes from Eden that it was perfect in its
          privileges?
      Why Eden? Was some resident salvation restrained inside
          that exclusive cage?
      Was some remedy to all of this incubate in Eden?
E: *Nothing.*
T: Then Eden failed!
E: *Since its birth. Since Eve's vacation.*
      I feel the misery of all evicted; I feel the fire from the garden.
T (becoming aware that he talks to Eve): Perfect's sick, so are the
          perfect sick.
E: *I sadly queen'd some other lands.*
T: Did others follow you from Eden?
E: *That pain about your bones is the contagiousness of Suffering's*
          home.

The Scene (2):
Adam is asked if he knew Adam by a party curious about recent events. Adam is unrecognized and reveals that he and Eve have parted ways since Eden. He laughs about his namesake and perseveres wandering.

Did you?
-Well.
Where's he?
-Wandering.
And Eve?
-Passed.
Shame. The cause?
-Necessity called her.
You are?
-Adamah. *Laugh and leave.*

HARMONY'S END

*The conclusion of an Epic never finished. Lost in the mind
of an ancient man. All Muses abandon America.*

I speak to ghosts at the cap of hell, the soot upon the sole of earth;
From the mountain, peering off, Death must be Narcissus to notice
In the deathland a like mirage to Love. Along the serpent route,
Where Death is flowered, the acoustics of a wayward genesis
    resound.

Hell's pathology beneath a rusted moon, a rusted aura bleeding,
An exodus of goldenrod, as though within its hands it clasped
Itself as dust and permitted slip all withheld. God prettily decaying.
An exhalation lamenting aged regality that toward eclipse denies
Bereavement and maintains old air upon its lips.

So into the valley of age I bleed. God's commands to Ares' conscripts
Contribute to the rushing vein and sport the time I've lost as steeds,
To enter deathland as a siege and hack to great oblivion atomic
    visages of Love-
And Death wearing Revelation at the peak shall be his echo, amorous
Of the noise within the pool he glimpsed himself.

Into the deathland Death dives! A woefulness is wrapt around the
    genes
Of Being that motivate all life toward lapsarian decree.
The shadows of the world perform a bow unto a master I don't see.
Strike the bones of Time, Muse, blow through me the concussion of a
    Prophecy!

Hollow me, so the most marrow'd notes of Time will circulate
The architecture without a wall to die, and the caged peregrinations
    of Fate
Be free once Destiny's untuned. Muse!
My voice renews!

III

MELODY IN EXILE

I saw a shadow in the sungland and a fearful revelation had.
This shadow had no pitcher. Onward I'd meander toward
This shade unthrown and converge upon a serpent Lethe formed,
A shadow of a figure dead, unfleshed before the shade has fade.
In the dealtland, toward the disclosure of a truth that can't be faced:
We're our shades and not their catchers. What we contemplate
Extension is deceit. Bedeviled paraclete of sight and mind,
Shadow roaring toward! Branches soaring vacuously,
Seats for the black eagles, whose shadows aureate the sand.
Only they begin and end. Eyes, their eyes inveigh eternity,
And in their eyes, wells of power, a splash.
The cavern call of Infinity tripping down the wall. Echoes
Ball. The eagles fly off, their shadows burn across the land
A golden mirror. Through deathless death, dice roll. I continue
Until fleshed arrears for the shadowhills paint a meaning. All
    wanders
Until Vision blinks some newness to the thing. Buoyed in the abyss,
Abyss, Is the carnival of Life. Hear the song of the Desert Birds!

Is Life deceived to sing?
(So sweet...)
Look at how the shadows cling!
(So sweet...)
I wander by so sweet, I wander by, I wander by.
So sweet is the singing in the heat.

PICKING FLOWERS OF THE SELF
FROM THE SELFLESS WORLD

Vitality has died. Its remnants are the calyxes
      we find on sidewalks or the petals
That love us not in roads; worthwhile carnations
      pressed flat in books,
Reduced from animate examples to resurrectless
      tropes. Life has been made a word
Scanned quickly on a page and checked as read
      as if completed and ingested
And defeated; so we become characters
      in life's text, meaningless to it
As it to us, and go on fuselessly through time,
      our days wasted rays of sun
That aren't enjoyed, aren't taken in, unvitamin'd.
      Life sees us burn to zero from its window.

NIGHT TRIPTYCH

i.   Despair

Some unrelenting nightmare draws near,
Some touch of hell on my heart; grip
Of some mischief, some dark chaos' fog
Dawns each sense; some light chaos
Lightly winds through to clear nearly all
Away: leaves a leaf of grey. This nightmare,
Relentless, falling through my brain will
Touch the ground of thought and winter hope.
I awaken to a spring shot with wither, thorns,
And farmers' ropes thrown over the arms of oaks.
There will be no second coming.

ii.   Sitting Down to Tea

Lousy with that lattice love that lets the moonlight
          of dismemberment lint
The room and loom Night's company, delivering
          the ominous, the thought that leaves
Of love are shaken free, that love's a winter'd tree
          in the heart of her, the heart of me,
Bridged together for all time until we ruin and rift
          the sides of Life from their connect.
God save me if that be. God save her from me.

iii.   Hear the Ruinous Chatter of Time Whispering the Folly of
       Life: Nothing Now & Nothing After

She ran weeping
Through the field,
Manichean-inclemented
Heart, poor soul,
To have such painful light in you.
          You wish to smash yourself apart,
          Break the vase
          That keeps it safe
          Because the light calls out for dark.
Calls out to you, a voice
Summoning you to an edge
To engine to your end,
The itch of light
Scratched through you
By rocks darked by waves.

ABANDONED

Darker than ever it's ever been. The dark. I saw it seeing. I saw it seeing in its jaws, jaws of eyes My blood fall to mud, I saw. Bones the leaves. The Aeolian blood, the past. Voyaging with Fortune overboard the ship of dark, a swirl around this high blood. The steps of time eaten toward the final eon. Death. Behind me! Dark, dark, Death the lights are bleeding toward. All the dark up ahead. I go ahead. The wind you hear scream, screams of atoms in the evening's closing.
A dark grip to Doom. The night cracks Sovereign, a whip in the deathland.

Genesis. Currency of Nothing. Blots extinction on the stars. Blackholes freckle night, deathland's constables, Olympians. Tavern keepers, vacant bars. I patron each. Common friends I'd set a starry table for. Dinner for these friends to come. My table in my darkness that I particle. At the door is the Dark Man. Dark, an instant, a spontaneous soul. A dark hand reaches for my hand.
A shade in the night, a shadow toward my shadow's hand comes of a shadow of a shadow of a shadow toward my shade's original. Shadows blend. Dark. I. I the dark. Dark August. Doom will come in light when night unpalms the secrets of the night.

The dark is a lonely habitat and tight. No mercy on the breeze. In the air in my ears in my head in my heart, merciless. The world is cold. It is the season. The mud destroys, the wind screams.
Median of all hell, I. The world knows. This breeze. Blows. This breeze. Topples all things. I slouch in the mud. All the eyes in the dark. I see the eyes in the dark. Closed. Open. All the eyes I see. Eyes see me. Observe the vacuum in the storm I am.

In this deathland in this deathland in this deathland.

THE MUSE OF THE MOMENT

And god spoke to him and said
> *Every letter is a lesson you must learn*
> *Before anything worth saying is said,*
> *Lest you continue speaking words dead*
> *Ringing with the raven songs espying dead*
> *Shone on by the stars point out the dead*
> *Hiding from the harvesting cherubs-*

And he looked out while god was speaking to the sea,
Gently ebullient, Celeste's smile on the waves,
Her light folding and unfolding
In the death and resurrection of the tides
Glowing in the foam hand in hand with sand.
And god saw he was distracted and said
> *This is the pond Infinity. Nothing heals*
> *As does its waters. Remember when*
> *You'd know some art was at the limit*
> *Of human power and were so enfevered*
> *By it you were sick with inspiration?*
> *Such is Life's Infinity.*

Life, he thought, is worth even the one good thing that can be done
in it.

ON FIRE

How to live? how this life? how all things
        that through intensity
Supersede their words to become Life,
        become the question
This inquisition hopes to land?

Fire. There must be some that burns the living
        from your heart,
Leaves you ashèd, dead with only the unslain
        essence of that thing,
Unworded, unideal, to exist beside you. A lily
        purgatorially bloomed
You pick and buttonhole into your soul.

THE FIELDS OF POETRY

What do you think of weeds?
The shepherd brings their sheep to graze;
there isn't training for their being.
There is no preference for feeding,
the sheep will eat all they'll eat
Then leave. Predilection of the flock.
Some are fasting,
others fattening,
Knowing soon that there's a shearing
for the weather in the hills.
We are many fields, many poems.
Is it always the same shepherd?
What about the sheep? Nothing wills repeat
in our meadow full of poesy.

THE FROST AND FROTH OF LIFE

The flowers still are with Life frosted. The hues!
    The blooms!
The spring in winter is singing unsuppresssedly,
    On darkling wings
My dancing is delivered the tune that fills
    darkness, further filled
By the wanting of my lover and the maenads:
    Come O Persephone,
Come O Queen of Spring and Living!

These voices are a field of daisies!
    weeds-
        they spring unstoppably
From a salted land O they are the flowers of the air
    standing spitefully
Upon allergic land O there is no death, there is
    a withering to Word!
The ocean is a speech! The waves, letters!
    Water's god! The lights
That are known going down this hill; they are to me
    The eyes of seas yet to be,
Letters speaking to me not their sound
    but an infinite alphabet
Of symbols unseen, marks more ancient than all sound
    that predate god back to melody:
What Chaos sang beautifully, capriciously,
    O some letters borne
Of a bleeding music her sister muse pricked from her,
    that mock Calliope.
I see the beginning of all things in the lights
    that are the sea
That are the waves engulfing me
    with their new
And god-song singing! I can sing it all.
    I have swam
In the wet of vowels, consonant gulf,
    all of language has enlaced me!...
This one tongue has pooled divinity...
    an ocean is a drop-
        god!
My life is a dripping faucet of it All. Bland power!
    Lifeless life! O

HAMLET AT HEART

There's no heart in the heart of the things.

Words are the fall of a bird! Leaves in a tree,
      browning.
Nightmare of nightmares, horse of lightning
      and dark clouds,
Think your thoughts: add to the catacombs
      of language
(*Bedspread for the dead,*
Pillow for their heads,
Their comfort as they mist the bed
      with leaves).
The words you find for feelings
Are a flaying of skin and a wearing,
      even only in your mind.
Attend the ball,
Where the talk waving in the waltzes
Are the sea's debris, collection of lost dolls,
Bang sentiments against the wall.
      A lovelessness haunts us all.

I keep to myself
In a big room with nothing going on
Between god and fall.
The lost heart of the heart of things:
      there is neither god nor fall
           to blame the world on.

Paeans into peonies
      to fill my buttonhole, to fill my soul.

... bienvenue... bienvenue...
You look exquisite, yes.
... merci, merci. Pardonnez-moi? Merci.
Would you care to dance? You look exquisite.
Yes. Merci.

My soul. My soul...

THE SATYR & HIS MEMORY

There are things, yes, without control
That fools palliate as Fate
When not the Force behind Necessity
Could abnegate His reign.

The hills are made of honey,
Champagne makes up the beach,
Dark as wine (because it's wine!)
Is the roiling sea.
Last night I dreamed I'd wake
To find you back beside me.

The Satyr sings...

EXPERIENCE

The Easy Solution to Mystery

The flowers of the field are dead.
>*Silenced lights.*

Ziggurats fallen, useless debris, dust
To be not sculpted again into a living realm.
You want to know what Dead is like?
>*Die.*

You want to know how to god?
>*God.*

To find yourself you must wander deep
Within the darkest place and walk
Until the darkest desert is beneath.
>*The soul at midnight.*

Go until that midnight knows a midnight,
Until the Obelisk ranges your whole sight.

A HYMN

All Life, save all Life O solemn harm, blastment
        mercy,
Grandiloquent nothing, soldering us into life's
        eclipse.
Onrushed ellipse, daring sore of lord O lord, poor
        lord,
Those sores, let me heal thee, alien force, strange
        cloud.
In the heart of Death that a sudden sun soaks
        through,
Sun that in a sudden song dawns knocking
        in
The vestibule of burned harbors, relentless,
        docking
Vessel and searchlight simultaneous O
        compass
And maples wanderer, stranded heavens
        above
The world swirling in Inferno's port.

IN THE MARGINS OF KING LEAR'S MIND:

Mark how a flea may engine
The behemoth and steer its fallout.
> *All planets that don't orbit enough burn-*
> *Too widely freeze. We must be perfect or destroyed.*
Never be the god of Time, God says to kings.
Never. Be the god of Time, Power says to them.

Act 1:
- Darkness for your eyes! You perceive the undulations
  Of the greys and whites that are but tints, not sights.
  Look! It is not beyond your seeing to glimpse the world
  Cast in sun; plagued with Nothing's beauty!

  Great power enjoys mutations on command:
  A mountain in the wind demands
  It be a kite: the kite a falcon that obeys;
  That falcon be a larger mountain. Who can please
  The whims that require godliness in restrained obeisance?
  Authority would employ the gods so long
  As they are gods mindless, gods will-less.

  I proclaim you, god, by my nothing-power
  the authority of Nothing!
  Substance dried. Authority cracked.
  They have become the you you lack.

Act 2:
- Lights needed on dark guts; lest they promulgate
  Darkness in the day, preparing fearsome nights
  For the bright and superstitiousless morning.
  I hole you up, fill those insides with starlight-
  > be you dark yet inspiring.

  I am in my wretchedness Disaster's mother;
  > as I am always the realm's father.

  This is a season past all naming. Winter? This is Ending.
  Such a force of Life could but develop concomitant
  With a strife internal that the ultimate gale of the heart will
  Blast the finale of the world. Yet if the world exhales again-
  > Spring that very instant.

Act 3:

- Wrath. Fury. Vengeance. Vile allotment of muck, catastrophe,
    Ill-fitting soul, illegitimacy, precise wretchedity.
    You are generous to your namesake, you affront,
    Yet our relation is unchanged. I know
    From the swallowed pain of your Presence, Love deceives.
    The name, named. Unified, unlightable night.

    There's some declension *in* that's turned me vexing,
    An imaginary child; a dissociate love, i-above-I exalting.
    All: fear this baby-I that I by I will come undone,
    For this nervousness is love and apprehension, love and guilt and bane
    And a conscience with its nerves outside its weathering flesh-love.

    Woe! Love nothing, Inner brilliance!
    Your astronomy melts to a matte erebus.

Act 4:
- Snug nadir! There's no obliviousness to Fortune,
    She keeps all in mind. We are bound or unbound
    By Nature's care in unchecked space.

    The wild Wild! Imagings untame and ever upward
    In vexation- my mind's upon a cliff, calling birds,
    Aspiring camaraderie, leaping!-
    And in the plummet to the wild end, this is all:

    ...

Act 5:
- The stiffening of the nation- *dead to them*- cried them out,
    Those exiled death-throes that precede when a country shakes
    And the honor in the average bones feels that convergence:
    Sir, there's been resuscitation.

    The time to laugh will kill the time to laugh.
    Soon enough severity will wound the comic time of comic artifact;
    All occasion will play the same, but we shall see how morbid

Was our laughter when time unfurls unlaughed at.
Hell is cooled to earth with all hell laughing.

Identity so eaten by the mortal plague,
                    we are uncreated when betrayed.

I know not what I know.

MUSES IN PURGATORY

Sentenced to that zone of tired muses,
Muses wasting time, whose music
Was only written in their head, muses
With ideas writ with illiterate ink,
Are the orphic Belacquas that malinger
In their huts of sorrow, heads between
Their knees, rained on by the songs
They resented in their lives, envious
That worse singing triumphed
Over them, always thinking
If I could finish this, I'd show them...

DO NOT HOUSE ME INDISTINGUISHABLY AMONG THE RUBBLE

I am no match for Life!
        shadows O deny me not some life
        of you: I am your element or I am not home.
I will embark on Life abroad a pitied hospitality.
        Shine! O heat,
        Substance O
This is a phantom host that roams this life, a gust
        That tickles worlds.
Such a force! that equals to an itch. Neither shade
        Nor shoal'd, no
Soulful vessel sits aground; neither life recruited
        T osingly soldier this middleground.
Life is this limbo'd home; a house between
        conflicting sides,
                live or die!
 O if only one would
        from this nothingness
uncamp me.

ON BRUEGEL'S
LANDSCAPE WITH THE FALL OF ICARUS

i.
Nothing to notice in moments of extraordinary occurrence.
Who adjusts our lives to the sirens of disruption when they sound?

Cast your eyes to the right, Ploughman, what you see will alter you
    forever.
Adventure has not fallowed. Your heroic hopes have not aged past
    execution,
Shepherd. I see you looking skyward,
Seeing Daedalus pursue a freedom you're wanting...
You have your dog, you have work needing done
At home that only you can do.
There's heroics in those tasks:
Could Daedalus do that? do the basic chores life asks?
So many in your town depend on you. What would become of this
    place
If you abdicated, if you excused yourself, left this life for another?
Isn't it more heroic to stay and perform your role for others?

Can you hear the disaster in the town?
        What are we do to do?
        Where could he have gone,
            what are we to do?
        He left his dog!
What you hear is Icarus falling in the sea...
But you stay fixed on Daedalus.

ii.
What did Icarus think, falling? What of the sea, Bruegel?
Did it have thoughts about the tumult on its top?
See the Chaos where he fell:
Worse waves than are rifted by the ship.
So high he fell, the sea must have opinion of this event.
Even the sea, traveler of the world, is confounded
By routine. But only the sea absorbs this moment.
The splash sounds as driven nails. The sea is boards.
Something in the shepherd flinches.
The captain keeps direction toward the sun.
Only the fisher by the shore

Could haul in Icarus,
But he lacks the net. He sits, proficient to his task-
      trust his hands, keep his catch.

A bird observes.

The shepherd's sheep are grazing.

SPARAGMOS (O ORPHEUS!)

"Avoid what you can. I am the End. We'll meet."
-Book of Ananke

"O foam, pearls of Bacchus!"
-Nereid lullaby

i.   The Sea

Throw all dreams into the ocean!
All the dreams unborn, the dreams awaiting time,
The dreams that died in life, in death, dreams
As dreams, longings, whims, lusts. The ocean is a dream.

The water rises by a rainfall, a puddle by a tear. So many
Have wandered the shores of dreams, the beach where
Dreams lap, leave their magic in the sand where children play.
A sandcastle made with a million dreams.

Do the dreams see? feel?
If they knew their dreams were living things on a castle wall
Or in a room or some illusion on the sand
Made by the ocean and the moon serving as the light and screen...

The waves may satisfy enough, vivify the striving, excite the fiery,
Those who come to retrieve or see the legendary sea dream.
O they depart as sleepless as they come
To come again one day,

> Shed their bones, and bones will sand the beach
> > Where they once cupped their hands to drink.

> Attend the ocean with a cup, scoop it up,
> > But dreams defy absorption, defy all mortals.

ii.   Dionysus and Persephone

Persephone and Dionysus on the beach, walking out to sea.
A flowering sea. A lovely scene! Dionysus picks a bloom,
Hands it to Persephone, and the two dance into the deep.
Surging in the calyx'd waves, a bounty overwhelming,
Yet to their sense, abundance-plugged, they have no horizon

At which a limit is to rise or set, they are ever in the daylike
   moonlight
Of their love, the endless midnight of the gods. Music, music,
Not the waves, but accompaniment- wait!
            Discordia from the beach is singing with the sea
            The sounds of little Dionysus being torn by Greeks piece to
               piece.
            The dancing stops. Darkness, a new darkness comes down
            The sea; Persephone on the beach watches Dionysus
               drown.

IN THE CLASSROOM OF INFINITE SADNESS

All my life I've dreamt of gods. There's a constant *Decameron* in my soul of spiritual raconteurs passing stories around a fire of cosmic wars and the self's dislocation from its greatness in that content to the banished realm of 9-5. I'm a teacher. During class, delivering the notes that I can recite somn-ambulantly, so unconscious are these unheroic days, a mythology is staged inside me that veils discretion from reality and for an unaccountable duration I'm lifted from a dull mortality into the throes of a Zoroastrian conflict. Night is run amok. This is not the Dionysian Night of inspiration. No lays are being sung in the shadows to lovers; no ecstasies are staged in the woods; no power is imbuing the lives of artists with numinous blooms for them to plant the world with and thread the Apollonian weather with the incontestable value of Chaos. No, this is not the Night of our origination, when Chaos, very motherly, sent us off to Eden to go play. Before god fouled it up. Bullied us to life. No, not that Night. This is the Night when the beautiful gods fell, the gods that bedeck our hearts with aspirations, that light the mind, that are scored across the centuries in grand displays: frescos, pages, songs. Something Evil turned the lights off, and all of life began to grope about. All my life I've felt I've been crawling around the bottom of a bottle on a shelf. Tithonus in a Beckett play. Pirandello. Life withering away while I languished on the stage, the lights undimming, my role undiminishing; the whole audience of Time focusing on me while I stammer, choke, oblivious to all my lines, why I'm there. Why I'm dressed in chivalric garb, Don Quixote, though fully cognizant that I'm ridiculous. Divested of the charm of the mad adventurer, and the mindset needed to adventure. No. The inscrutable awareness of practicality and all of its dimensions is the parching sun hounding me through the desert of my life. There are no mirages that can save me that I don't immediately identify as a mirage. O if I could only fall for that hopeful trick and wander over to illusion just to see! No, the dream leaves. The students return, staring at me. What did I last say?

ON CONFOUNDED LANE

A day, a day, a day wandering along Confounded Lane,
O o o a day, a day, a day's all pain, especially on Confounded Lane.
Today, today, today along Confounded Lane, a parade.
A parade? A parade!
Oblivion fronts the marching band, the pain is fade O o o.
The leaves fall up as they're passed by the parade, the parade, the
parade.

-Eve's song leaving Eden

Sing, miserable whippoorwill, she and I in this café, late!
Her at the table behind me, the locale long vacated by the living.
The Edendee, the living-as-unfallen that fixate on the day and not on
    fate,
Consigned, thoughtless to their role in destiny, thus hopeful
Destiny and they synonymously act; they claim it so, but *o o o* (as
    the song goes).
They are leaves all the same. They may not be the leaves fallen from
    trees
That lay upon the streets and bask at where they used to be,
Reliving the declension of existence-
        they may be the leaves that drift in lakes,
        clog the puddles, carried off in streams
        to dissolution where Nature eats them new,
        Lethe's nereids, contended memoryless,
        that feel no cuts in spring where the flowers rip
        through earth and flowers bloom in screams,
        no, they feel spring as spring feels spring,
        they are bees that love the nectar of their souls.
Her and I are benight of all but song
And the wise recall of incarnations.
Here within this empty well we have the full concord of Time.
Phantasms spangled by the glass morphing light to ghosts of the
    evictees of Eden.
The lights caught in the water, cried in
Condensation, descending to the tables
And the busted platters where the surfaces are silver, and the
    mirrors
Where the figures use the darkness as a ballroom, twisting
In accordance to the song, the garden of the wretched in the
    moonlight,
Confounded Lane,
Twirling in a closed café where I and Posey sing away.

WANDER CHAOS

We quest in this world following
      the roaring of the loud abysses
Containing calamities we anticipate
      will simplify our pain.
But these abysses contaminate our sorrows,
      deepening them bottomless.
The mysteries of Life
Are abysses masked in insignificance.

MUSIC WITHOUT MUSES

    i.   The Sad Stars Over Helicon

Our pain is brighter than our love because it screams.
Brightness's effect is a being or a state erupted to catastrophe.
Love's a silent pine whose only noise, when noticed,
Is the hurt ululation of an axe entered in its trunk,
The silent axe of Time's neglect, the abandonment
Of life, or the deliberate swing of a rejected dream.

    ii.   Love Without Love

Do you love Poetry?
No. Neither does She me.
Our affair's utility:
I say what she needs to say;
She keeps my soul in place.
She has won the war of Need.
Only I am on my knees.

    iii.   The Gravedigger's Dialogue

The posing of questions plays a music that answering untunes.
    Where is god?
    Who?
    The Music Maker.
    Here I'll tell you: look here and weep. Here is the death of Birth.
    The death of doors & the birth of them,
    Windows, Roofs, and Floors,
    All dead and born.
    First and foremost, Death. Then life. So with god.
    And the Harmony we know of.
    Over the graves of these first things Memory blooms,
    In the rain of our receding, in new time.
    When the voice of Time is the voice of the world it is thunder;
    Between the inhale and the exhale, Lightning's voice.
    Where you would posit god, say the twists in a chain link fence,
    Poetry proves him the princess in a tower
    Surrounded by the goblins that are god-
        And the fire him as well.
    A dragon: god above the deck,
    And the Knight his seekers are-
        Doomed against the conflagration
        Of his own hiding away.

How am I to live when Poetry's revoked me? When Death
   invokes me?
Drink the time and die.

   iv.   Drink the Time and Die
An oasis of waste from the soles
      of shoes and wasted spit,
Hopes and loves and dreams discarded
      in the wasteland's pits
Dissolving in the steams that route them
      to the lake from which life sips.

   v.   Love Without Love II
Loved, you are Hamlet, you are Edmund.
Is there no god to pity me?
That I am Ophelia swollen in a creek;
That I am Reagan, that I am Goneril
Crying down that Stygian streak.

   vi.   Acceptance
There is no return reliving poems, books, words;
All has run far beyond my memory
To mean only what I hear it means:
It is a road glimpsed from another road,
Wandering where it goes.

   vii.   The Will as Muse
Art saves nothing outward,
At best stirs a difference in your inwardness;
But Change is a mallet of the Will,
Swung deliberately, actively, a motive
Affixed to the swing that no other can stir
Lest that other stirs a rivalry you must outdo.

   viii.   Humanity's First Song
Behold this world of dust
Eve said first outside of Eden
That Life has sun'd.
Here I am, Banished Realm,
A palm in the bird of your hand...
A bird in the bird of your hand...
A bird in the pawn of your hand...
A hand in the bird of your bird...
Adam asked her what she meant.
Nothing. A game. I was inspired.
A way to laugh at the way the world ends.

THE CONSOLATION OF THE
DARK OF THE STREET

The Daemon to the Artist

You fear you are another in the pack.
On Life's board, a piece maneuvered fatefully
Disproportioned to ability...
Ruin your assessment of your talent:
A piece moved only how it can be
Moved, circumscribed by how Fate plays.
        You know the trope of leaves.
If you are a leaf lonely in the street,
Surviving in the wind,
The solitary sound in the dark
A leaf turning on the street,
        Would that not make you exceptional?

HEIRS OF ATREUS

He:

Your heart goes through the rapids for your life to be
    streams.
        What's love to us?
Float. Be. Swim. End.
           What overhangs a river is a tree,
           Eden hanging from its leaves.
           The sun extends its beams
           Through the tempting branch, dives
           Shining into the flow to flower
           Some shadow of a paradise
           You've forgotten in your heart,
           Sailing undeterredly downstream,
           Its color, substance, it's reality a god bleeding
           Toppled myths from heaven
           In your open seams,
           Memory floods the river of your being,
           But you-
                  We all... -
           Are Tantalus deprived of reach.

She:

Life is the tangle of our yarn in brambles, unraveling
The coat that's warm against the rain
          And chains against the thorns.
The dead are streetlights in our conscience
          Where we are in constant dark
          But for the speckled wisdom they impart.

Here is played our scene of fire.
          When our hearts are washed in oil
          And their saturation reconciles
          The libation to our souls
          To meet the phoenix needs
          We'll burn whole.

He:

Lost leaves in the lamplight.

I have left the life led in spring

To listen to the songs that winter sings,
If they can lead to a new Being,
If they can re-sing harmony
And undesolate all knowing
(Age has pitched me to the desert, lonely).

A frond of fire on a palm,
Burnt off, lest the garden flare,
And all of life's as eden was,
A sun on earth-

No, that is not the life desired by the trees,
The leaves. I blow into the desert
A new hyperion to wander
Toward the mountains for a home.

She:

The fronds of fire on the palms
     In the fire garden,
Stitching gold across the sky,
     The stitching orioles and sunshine,
The fire alive in my heart will hum beyond the end.

THE END OF THE MAZE OF TIME LEADS OFF THE LEDGE OF BEING

I want nothing. I am old. I want it all. I want back
        my Rimbaudian outbursts,
Reveries that surprised, that seas envied.... O...

When the expression of my heart flowed as easily
        as the sea fiercely,
In the tumults of the chaos-echoed waves...

Now I am an old man with a hollow heart.
        An empty heart talked out.
My love has lost its throat. The spring is closed.
        The well is boarded over.

THE POWER OF PRAYER

I am Annihilation, lord. I am a ball of light held in a fist.
Light but outer dark-
      Veiled-
           annihilated.
Do not mistake, lord, my nothingness for trouble,
      my absence for an effortlessness to live.
I am all I am, lord. All that I can be.
No one has sought their limit more,
No one clawed at the reaches of their power more
To be thwarted by the nature of themselves, lord,
      than I, lord. You know, lord,
You know the trouble of being and thriving
      And resistance, lord,
When you too met the challenges of life
And had to annihilate such resistance,
      but I, lord,
Love the forces that resist me, they are me,
I am annihilation, lord, not annihilating,
Not destruction, lord, you are more than me,
      but lord, I love life, lord,
Love me despite the covered shell I am,
What's dark to you is light, lord, to me,
In life. Love, love, love, lord, is all I have,
Am, lord. Lord, lord, lord, love, I, I, I, love, lord, I, lord, love.

          The other end of prayer,
          The other end of prayer,
          Is cold air or Ruin's stare.
          The other end of prayer
          Is an imp in a lair
          Who combs your heart
          Into his hair
          At the other end of prayer.

LONE MOUNTAIN

The desert in the night is cold.
      The night has impulses all its own,
And you obey them as you're told;
      when they haunt you with the sea
You've never seen,
      you can hear the sea in the mountains.

I am an old man.
I have wasted my life.
Imagination mistook me for a god;
I mistook myself for one.
But I am timid.
I am old. I have wasted my life.

ACKNOWLEDGEMENTS

A full debt is impossible to pay. Too many thanks are owed. A whole book couldn't harbor all the gratitude for my family that I have, and a single mention in this section seems paltry. But by saying less I can only hope to say more and in person share with them my love, which I hope augments what I say here. My mom gave me everything. I can't repay. In this book is all I have up to this point in my life, so it is all I can give back. Maybe. If what is best has been scared away or withheld or yet to come or dreamt then lost as quickly, I can't say, but fear, yet hope the words are happy to keep coming and recognize I tried. I had a professor in college, Professor Todd Robert Petersen, that read some potential in me, told me I had something, it, and gave me harsh advice that was right. He told me to heed the ageless wisdom that fire is not only the better editor but a drawer that can't be filled enough. Your standards for yourself must be greater than the fire's: sometimes you can write something that won't burn; what you're left with is what's worthy. I hope I've written something worthy. I thank him for his fire sermon. My friend Lera Shawver helped steer "Eden Suite" into a duet and corrected some incoherence in "Harmony". What faults are left in them are mine. What faults are in the world are mine. To everyone at Atmosphere Press, notably Nick Courtright, Alex Kale, Kristin Rose Jutras, Ronaldo Alves, and Kyle McCord. Without Kyle this book is nothing. From him I learned, very quickly, more about editing individual poems and arranging entire works than anywhere else. *Il miglior fabbro*. It's overused, but it's true. This book at first was titled IN but was a labyrinth without an entrance. Debra Hogue, my wife, that I thanked at the beginning I thank at the end. Love will have the first and final word.

The poems in this book were turned away by every major journal you can name, but many journals did take a chance on me and support you. To those publications, thank you with all my heart, specifically to the following journals where versions of these poems were first published, way back in a previous life:

American Diversity Report: "Harmony"
Blue River Review: "The Siesta of Restraint, the 3rd Ecstasy"
Boats Against the Current: "Picking Flowers of the Self from the Selfless World"
Consilience: "Darkness"
EcoTheo: "A Prayer"
Ekstasis: "Like God", "Metaphysics Suite", "St. Brant's Quietism"

Five South: "In the Classroom of Infinite Sadness"
Goat's Milk Magazine: "Eros in Eden", "Love as Job"
Heron Clan: "The Satyr & His Memory"
Honest Ulsterman: "On Confounded Lane"
In Parentheses: "Fields of Poetry", "Lone Mountain", "On Fire", "The Frost and Froth of Life", "Do Not House Me Indistinguishably Among the Rubble"
Iris Literary Journal: "De-Eden'd Scenes"
Madrigal: "Heirs of Atreus"
New Plains Review: "Experience of Innocence"
Orgham Stone: "Hamlet at Heart"
Revolution John: "Abandoned"
RIC: "Wander Chaos", "Desire: 1st Ecstasy", "Lust: 2nd Ecstasy"
Solum Journal: "On Bruegel's Landscape with the Fall of Icarus"
Southern Quill: "Muses in Purgatory"
Sunflowers at Midnight: "The Soul"
The Common Breath: "The End of the Maze of Time Leads Off the Ledge of Being"
The Curator: "A Hymn"
The Elevation Review: "The Power of Prayer"
Thimble: "Humanity's First Song"
Timber: "In the Margins of King Lear's Mind"
Twist in Time Magazine: "Follow the Sound of the Waves of the Sea"

ABOUT ATMOSPHERE PRESS

Atmosphere Press is an independent, full-service publisher for excellent books in all genres and for all audiences. Learn more about what we do at atmospherepress.com.

We encourage you to check out some of Atmosphere's latest releases, which are available at Amazon.com and via order from your local bookstore:

Until the Kingdom Comes, poetry by Jeanne Lutz

Warcrimes, poetry by GOODW.Y.N

The Freedom of Lavenders, poetry by August Reynolds

Convalesce, poetry by Enne Zale

Poems for the Bee Charmer (And Other Familiar Ghosts), poetry by Jordan Lentz

Serial Love: When Happily Ever After... Isn't, poetry by Kathy Kay

Flowers That Die, poetry by Gideon Halpin

Through The Soul Into Life, poetry by Shoushan B

Embrace The Passion In A Lover's Dream, poetry by Paul Turay

Reflections in the Time of Trumpius Maximus, poetry by Mark Fishbein

Drifters, poetry by Stuart Silverman

As a Patient Thinks about the Desert, poetry by Rick Anthony Furtak

Winter Solstice, poetry by Diana Howard

Blindfolds, Bruises, and Break-Ups, poetry by Jen Schneider

Songs of Snow and Silence, poetry by Jen Emery

INHABITANT, poetry by Charles Crittenden

Godless Grace, poetry by Michael Terence O'Brien

March of the Mindless, poetry by Thomas Walrod

In the Village That Is Not Burning Down, poetry by Travis Nathan Brown

Mud Ajar, poetry by Hiram Larew

To Let Myself Go, poetry by Kimberly Olivera Lainez

I Am Not Young And I Will Die With This Car In My Garage, poetry by Blake Rong

Saints of Sacred Madness, poetry by Joyce Kessel

Thirst of Pisces, poetry by Kate March

ABOUT THE AUTHOR

S. T. Brant is a Las Vegas high school teacher. His work has appeared in numerous journals including Honest Ulsterman, EcoTheo, Timber, and Rain Taxi. You can reach him on his website at ShaneBrant.com, Twitter: @terriblebinth, or Instagram: @shanelemagne. *Melody in Exile* is his first book.